# MYSTIC MINA

My Life

Love

and

Lessons

as

An Empath

By

*Isha' Mina*

© Copyright (2021) by (Isha' Mina) - All rights reserved.

It is not legal to reproduce, duplicate, or transmit any part of this document in either electronic means or printed format. Recording of this publication is strictly prohibited.

I turned my pain from the past into life lessons

I appreciate I'm no longer in the spaces I dwelled in

I'm grateful for this opportunity of sharing

# Table of Contents

**TABLE OF CONTENTS ................................................. IV**

**INTRODUCTION ........................................................... 1**

CHAPTER ONE: MYSTIC MINA ........................................... 5
CHAPTERTWO: BLACK GIRL MAGIC ................................ 13
CHAPTER THREE: THAT 11 LIFE ..................................... 21
CHAPTER FOUR: JUST AN INFJ ...................................... 28
CHAPTER FIVE: NOTHING BUT LOVE .............................. 36
CHAPTER SIX: DANCING WITH THE DEVIL .................... 43
CHAPTER SEVEN: CLUB CLOWNING ............................... 50
CHAPTER EIGHT: IN HERMIT MODE ............................... 55
CHAPTER NINE: BEING SAFE IN YOUR SHADOWS ........ 65
CHAPTER TEN: THE GIFT IN GRATEFULNESS ............... 73
CHAPTER ELEVEN: HEALED FROM MY MOTHERS PAIN
........................................................................................ 76

**CONCLUSION .............................................................. 82**

**ACKNOWLEDGMENTS .................................................. 85**

**ABOUT THE AUTHOR .................................................. 86**

# Introduction

I have always felt different, but I never understood why. I was timid and quiet. I would constantly be in my head thinking a lot, and people labeled me stuck up or feeble-minded due to that. I never ran with the popular crowd because I was always very comfortable with being by myself. Growing up in the hood, I noticed I felt deeply, more than most. I have always been in touch with my emotions. I have always been empathetic, and others took that as a sign of weakness. I always had a gift of knowing without knowing what being intuitive was. I always loved animals without a cause. People always confided in me with their life journeys, and I didn't understand why. Even though I have always been shy, I always would stand out in the crowd. Even through my mistakes and mishaps in life, I have been big on integrity, and the times I ignored it, I suffered greatly. Even though I'm an introvert, creativity flows through me naturally. I was hiding behind many things like routine jobs, people-pleasing, and self-sabotaging throughout the years of my life. This is my story about how I am living in the truth of my greatness.

## Chapter One: Mystic Mina

You know that one girl who wants to know your birthday, the one who loves astrology, numerology, crystals, altars, plants, animals, spirituality, believes the moon affects people, Universal Law, the power of love, and the divine gift of intuition. Well, she is me all day, every day. Growing up, I always felt more connected to what most people didn't even acknowledge or took for granted. I have always been aware of myself, even when I tried to ignore parts of my true self.

Way before YouTube, Instagram, and TikTok, I have always been into astrology. Back when the only way you could read your horoscope was in the daily newspaper or the popular magazines. Way before the ShadeRoom, they had magazines that specialized in black music and culture. When I found out that Al B. Sure sun sign was a Gemini, I was so

# Mystic Mina

excited. I loved astrology because it gave me the key to learn about different people without really knowing them, an introvert's dream. The mostly used Astrology is the Western Astrology but there are other forms of Astrology that people practice around the world like the Native and Chinese. Even though some don't believe astrology, it plays a part in many things. The world's most successful people will have their own paid astrologist right by their side.

The power of the moon is fantastic. The wolf doesn't howl at the moon for nothing. I know there are a lot of people who don't believe in "moon magic." Still, I'm sure anyone reading this that works with the public, especially police officers and emergency rooms workers, can attest to the full moon bringing something out of people that makes their occupation extremely interesting. You're probably wondering why the moon does certain things to people. The easiest way I can explain is energy. The moon increases power in people and animals, and sometimes that can be good or bad. Like the wolf knows he is a wolf, but when the full moon comes out, the wolf has let all the animals know he is a wolf, too. If that makes sense. Many crimes are committed during the full moon also. When you have an individual functioning at a lower frequency than full moon will intensify that, or, if you are an energetic person, the full moon may make you anxious, if you don't release that energy. Still, the moon intensifies your energy so much that if it's not released correctly, it can make you feel out of sorts. I usually chill out during a full moon, especially in South Central LA. Whenever there is a full moon, I will relax with some feel-good music, light some candles, take a long bath, journal my emotions and speak my affirmations.

When it comes to spirituality, I always felt more connected to that spectrum of practice. The spirit has existed way before any religion, so it was much easier for me to connect directly to the Source. In no way is this a reason to bash anyone else religious beliefs. Especially since there are over 4000 types of religious groups and spiritual traditions in this world, it's not up to me to decipher whether any religious practice is right or wrong. If there are any practices, a community adheres to and that brings them closer to their GOD, then more power to them. I will not degrade any for their beliefs, and I don't want anyone to belittle me for mine.

    Even though I consider myself more spiritual, I adhere to quite a few things that will come from certain religions. When a co-worker of mine passed away, another co-worker asked if I was familiar with this tradition. I wasn't but I was glad she discussed it further. Everyone will meet at the altar, for the one who passed away, filled with pictures, food, and flowers. Then for a whole week, people will come by to give their offerings to the deceased, and on the 7th day, everybody will gather at this altar with letters and prayers for the dead to have an easy transition to the other side. I thought that was beautiful, especially from a culture where altars and connecting with your ancestors are deemed unnecessary and evil.

Speaking of evil, I have heard so many things concerning crystals deeming them evil. But this logic never made any sense to me. Crystals are natural resources like gold, diamonds, oil, and water. They come directly from Mother Earth. Things are not evil; however, the intentions that someone puts into a thing can make it appear that way. For example, if you had a hammer and hit someone with it, does that make the hammer evil or the person handling it? That same hammer in the hands of someone with good intentions can help someone build instead of breaking people down. Different crystals have healing properties, but the true power comes from the person handling the crystal. Just because you have a rose quartz stone representing love, beauty and femininity does not mean you will automatically receive the benefits from that stone. Studies have shown that people have found ordinary rocks while walking that they put their intentions into and receive the same

# Mystic Mina

healing properties. All in all, the power relies upon you, not the object.

With animals and nature, well, I guess that goes without saying. A majestic tree, a flourishing plant, and a bed of roses filled with ladybugs, bees, and butterflies define what true beauty is. And for the animals, I always loved and admired them. A good night for me will be with puppy videos, lions in the wild, or just a great episode of neo geographic. Even stray animals will find their way to me. I remember one day, a little dog followed me on my lunch break during my walk, looking as if he wanted me to take him home. He must have felt I was a sucker for animals, and if I weren't at work, I would've taken him home with me. But thankfully, he attached to someone else while my walk was over. Or that time someone violently, hit a dog, racing down my residential street. Thankfully, many people called animal control, but they went directly into their homes as soon as they finished the call. But not me. I stayed outside until Animal Patrol came, usually, that could up to 3-4 hours, but I didn't mind if they did. Luckily, they came in about an hour, and I went inside after they were gone. I couldn't imagine anyone, or animal left on the street left alone.

I even try to live life by the universal laws without really knowing what they were at a time. I remember being in Ms. Simmon's class in 4th grade, and we used to sing the golden rule, and even to this day, that song is forever embedded in my memory. Even though that reference is in the book of Matthew, all I can hear is her singing it 'Life is really like a rule, the olden golden rule, do unto others as you want them to, do unto you." I always understood the energy you put out you will receive.

Duality is a part of life, as above so below, as the law of polarity. All people have a duality between the masculine (thinking) and feminine (Feeling) and understanding negative −and positive things is part of this duality. I always did what I would want in return for others, but when people live on the other side e of that spectrum, reciprocation is not on the board. I have even been in a few situations where people got mad at me because I didn't join in the conversation of judging and belittling people.

Now I am far from a saint, there have been times when I let my anger get the best of me, and I had to regret the words that came out of my mouth. I'm not perfect, but I try to refrain from that activity because I understand how I'm judging someone; someone else can judge me the same way. I believe that many people don't look at it that way because everyone wants to be perfect and pointing out someone else's flaws makes them feel justified in a way. Misery loves company.

## Chapter Two: Black Girl Magic

I was born a Lovechild in the early 80s on Diana Ross's birthday, raised in South Central LA, in the middle of the wars on gangs, drugs, and poverty, as an Empath. It may sound, a little ironic. Let's be honest a "hood empath" sounds like a title from a BET film, but it is, what it is. Of course, growing up, I had no idea what being an empath was or any clue I was one myself. I just knew I felt certain things, but I was unaware that everybody else didn't.

"An 80s baby", my world wasn't filled up with that many labels, and I appreciate that because a child that's an empath will not participate or engage themselves in ways an average child would. And that, especially in society today, will leave a child excessively labeled. A lot of empaths are introverts, and they are emotionally aware. A child like this is very observant and typically wants to avoid unnecessary situations even at a very young age. A child that is an Empath can come off withdrawn and non-verbal at certain times or situations I hardly spoke, but I was very aware.

My mother will often reminisce on how around 4, I started reading everything from signs to billboards, I love to read, and nothing has changed today. I remember those long talks my mother and brother used to have, and I would just sit there to soak up all the free games they were giving. Sometimes I would say my two cents, and that was rare. Same thing with school, I was a great student, and I always received good grades on my report card along with the notation that I needed to be more involved in-class activities. I was timid and quiet. Sometimes that can be seen as something different because an empathetic child is observant and will process the environment and conditions before putting themselves into a situation.

Let's take an elementary school filled with children, for instance. And now it's time for recess. Everybody knows how play breaks look. Kids will be running, jumping, playing, and shouting everywhere. Doing what kids do and only focused on the main objective, having fun. But there is one child that is doing the complete opposite. This child observes everybody and everything to see where they fit comfortably in the situation, unbeknownst to the child. Let's just say this child sees an unattended ball and decides they want to play with that ball but notices their classmate Paul has the ball, now and this child has a dilemma. Do they ask Paul to play with this ball or find something else? But now Susan wants to take the ball from Paul, and now a fight has started. Now all the kids are gathering around because they are fighting over the ball. The empath child will choose to forget the ball because they don't want to be a part of the commotion and turn around and hop on a bike; the other kids stopping riding and enjoy playing alone.

To some, that situation may look like the child disengaging from their peers. Still, the child was aware of their surroundings, decided that the ball wasn't worth the fight that came with it, and made a sound choice to find something else to play with that made them happy, and their choice wouldn't leave them emotionally disturbed. That child was me.

I guess you are wondering, "OK, girl, what's an Empath?" An empath is a highly compassionate person that is aware and tuned in with the emotions of others and the activities around them to the point where they can become overwhelmed or influenced emotionally and physically, all due to their surrounding environment. If someone is having a bad day comes around an empath, instantly they can find themselves attuning to that same energy. Or if someone is sick, some empaths can feel and experiences the same ailments as someone close when there is absolutely nothing wrong with them. Lying to someone who feels other people's emotions is like lying to yourself because we can see right through it, even when we pretend, we don't at times. Being an Empath person isn't a cut-and-paste prototype. Experiences can differ from one Empath to the next. Some will experience things on a more profound level than the next, but every Empath is unique in its own divine right.

Growing up in the hood as an empath can be challenging. I would be rich today if I got paid for every time someone called me bougie or stuck up because I was quiet or a loner. I was always the one who was friends with the popular one, but never the popular one, and I was OK with that. With me always being so intuitive, I was very observant. Some people will speak only when they need to and not because they can. You will never catch me being the loudest in the room because I'm checking out my environment, the people in it, the conversations, what people do or don't say while focusing on the energy. I can walk into a room and immediately pick up on the aura throughout it. That is the very reason why being in the popular crowd or clique was never my thing. I prefer to know someone on a more genuine, intimate level rather than being amongst the popular group idolizing people over their material possessions. Even in dating, I always liked the lowkey person, the one who wasn't confined with what everyone else was doing.

Being an empath requires intense selections of one's environment setting. If ignored, that can have an empath feeling drained, stressed, depressed, or in pain, all from just mirroring the energies surrounding them. That's why romantic or platonic relationships can be very draining for an empath if they are unhealthy. Being so intuitive, we often can see and know things people will try to hide from others, without trying. Boundaries are essential for an empath because we often want to make sure everyone around us is OK, even if it means ignoring our own needs. Loyalty and dedication aren't just words for an empath. It is a way of life. If you have an empath in your life, you will always have someone to depend on. An untrained empath will allow anyone to come into their world because we can empathize and sympathize with literally anyone needing assistance. So much, we can easily fall for the classic narcissist. A narcissist wants nothing more than to receive what the empaths give, and an unhealed empath wants nothing more than share what a narcissist is missing. It's a toxic tango for sure.

I guess that's why people approach me because of my gift of empathy; whether it is strangers on the street, the person talking to themselves at the bus stop, or just people with many accolades and accomplishments, they will all approach me. Empaths can be that flame that a moth is attracted to unknowingly. Before I understood what an empath was, that aspect used to leave me puzzled. Like, "Why are people are approaching me and asking me these questions? or Why are they talking to me?" If it's a crowd of people around, someone will single me out for conversation. But now I understand because reasoning, understanding, and connecting with others intuitively come naturally to me. Being able to relate to someone without being in that situation is what I do naturally. Like I stated before, I was never in the "in crowd" but you will be surprised about all the drama and secrets I know about during school, just sitting back in silence, observing.

Nature is fundamental to me because, as an empath, we appreciate things that money can't buy, the simpler things in life. The beauty of nature is fascinating. I always feel more connected to the Source. I lived 5 minutes from the beach at one point in my life, and I walk to it every day. Being so close to one of nature's gifts, just feeling the sand in between my toes, the breeze of the ocean, and the sound of the water waves felt so serene. Even as a child, I connected to animals, and they tend to attach themselves to me. Dogs love me; no pun intended. Everything from flowers, birds, bees, trees, butterflies, and ladybugs bring me immediate joy. To this day, it's a flock of birds that have claimed my rooftop as their home, but I don't mind their good morning tweets are like music to my ears.

# Chapter Three: That 11 Life

So, Alice Walker, Nivea, Tyler Perry, Tony Robbins, and I have one thing in common. We share the Life Path number 11. According to numerology, if you have a birthdate, you also have a life path number. It's a form of astrology but with numbers. There are many people who are very successful numerologists who also study the energy of numbers, like an astrologist checking the placements and degrees of astrology. You can find your number by adding your birthday down to its most simplified number except the numbers 11, 22, 33; these numbers shouldn't be reduced because they have a special meaning. Your life path number gives you a synopsis of what your life path will be. Of course, your personal decisions and your destiny will be up to you in your right. But your life path number can help explain why you value, think, love, or are emotionally invested in things naturally. Your life path number will show you a better glimpse of yourself, if needed, like your zodiac sign.

    I guess you are wondering what a Life Path number 11 consists of being. It has been noted and proved that number 11's are intensely intuitive, extremely informative, innovators, and the world's healers. Some people have this life path number and have chosen to act and live on the other side of the spectrum. There will be polarity for everything; for every Ying, there's a Yang. For example, Will Smith and Tupac Shakur both are successful entertainers, who you can clearly see or like night and day, but they both share the same life path number 22. You will always find an 11 to look to for love, healing, or inspiration for the most part. Whether it is as common as encouraging losing weight or starting a garden, starting a business venture, or making a move to another country, and 11 will be there to give you a push with a lot of guidance attached to it.

    That is the significant part of being an 11, that all these things come to you naturally. It's the divine

Mystic Mina

birthright of intuition and love that is in us. But an unhealed number 11 can endure a tremendous amount of pain in a lifetime by always letting the needs and desires of other people overshadow their own. If we decide to expand our gifts with personal education. That structure and root of a healer and teacher will always be in place. That is the main reason you find number 11's in career paths as a lecturer, prolific writer, political activist, psychic, artist, philosopher, and musician.

      Like I stated before, that could be the very reason why people in my life will confide their information with me and ask for my opinion. I guess my aura will have people come to me for my advice without them even noticing it. I know there are times when people need someone just to listen and vent. I always made myself available to listen, but mainly I'm concerned about solutions. As a life path number 11, I'm very optimistic, and in life, I always focused more on correcting the issue than on the subject. If you live this thing called life, you will face obstacles, but what many people do is focus on this problem, and in return, it becomes a bigger problem. Some people will choose to stay in their problems and blame them, not realizing it's a personal choice (when you are an adult) to remain in an unhealed life situation. With the proper tools and solutions, problems will be something you just have to overcome and not a state of being.

Thanks to the land of fake reality shows of dysfunction, money-hungry individuals, being in drama, ready to fight at a drop of a dime will always get you the most attention. It will keep you trending, you will be blog-worthy, and people will either love you or love to hate you. Like in the entertainment world, bad publicity is still publicity. Energy is a massive revolving door, so what you participate in and attune your energy to will eventually grow bigger or start manifesting physically in your life.

One thing about manifesting, it doesn't matter what you say you don't want; it only pays attention to the energies you are participating in, whether it is for a check or social status. People will only be able to understand and develop as far as they can see. That's why I don't fret when I share my thoughts and people aren't ready to receive them. The answer always lies within oneself anyway. So, if you feel that nothing will change, this is your life, whether good or bad. Then that is what you will receive.

As a life path 11, I learned that I am not here to fix but only assist. That is where problems will arise is when people like me will try to "fix" someone. In reality, fixing someone is impossible. Because if you had the power to change anyone around you, then it will be done. But whether someone is living right or wrong, everyone has the free will to live the way they decide. It is only up to you to determine if you want to involve or participate in their way of life or choice. If you do, so be it; if you don't, then let it be.

Actual change comes from within and not from another person's hand. I now understand that people

## Mystic Mina

have a hard time digesting this because it's difficult for some to realize why they are or aren't in their lives. Once you are an able-minded adult, you can make confident choices in life, and those choices will lead to specific circumstances. And within those circumstances, if you like the outcome, continue that path, but if you don't like the result, you change the direction. It is insane to want different results doing the same thing. To get something you always wanted, you must do something that you have never done.

Being a life path number 11, I understand that happiness is a state of being and not a condition of having. People like me cherish the simpler things in life, like, laughter, love, memories, peace, music, and nature. Material things can be bought, destroyed, and bought all over again but there are certain things in life that money can't buy. Whether you know an 11 who is living a life full of material riches or just a modest everyday life, they will always take time to adhere and enjoy the things that's closest to their heart.

# Mystic Mina

# Chapter Four: Just an INFJ

I know I mentioned I'm a little bit of everything. Being an introvert, I was curious about learning new things about the world and myself. I felt like I was the oddball out because I was always more interested in what's within. I love researching new things, reading books, and watching documentaries. But there is nothing more satisfying than self-discovery to me.

So, during a rabbit hole session, I discovered something out there called MBTI, which stands for The Myer-Briggs type indicator. The MBTI is an assessment tool that breaks down psychological functions of sensations, intuition, feeling into different categories. And these categories produce 16 MBTI types. There are various assessment tools online that you can use to determine your personality type, but the original one is about 90 questions long. There are no right or wrong answers to these questions because they are only needed to determine your MBTI type, and no type is a "wrong" type. Some types are prevalent, but one type is scarce, according to this assessment tool. And that type is INFJ, and I discovered that I was that type.

"What's an INFJ?" First, the INFJ stands for (I)Introversion, (N)Intuition, (F)Feeling, and (J) for Judgment. Introversion is about being introverted. While INFJs can easily be seen as extroverts because the last half Feeling and Judgment is on extroverted sensation. As for me, I could very much seem extroverted in different situations where I find passion and pleasure.

You will find me either with some earphones, reading, writing, dancing, or singing. That's because I don't talk a lot, and everybody needs a form of self-expression, even if it's not verbal. I have always understood and loved the power of being silent, but if you do find me speaking, you better listen because I don't talk just to talk; it will always have substance behind it. That is another thing about having one of the rarest personality traits. Meaningless conversations are

## Mystic Mina

dreadful to someone like me. It's only so much celebrity gossip I can tolerate. Being an INFJ, I love diving into the deep end of the pool regarding conversations about love, life, and everything in between. People like me know the power in silence and only speak when it is necessary.

The intuition aspect kind of goes hand and hand with introversion. Being an introvert leaves me alone with my thoughts all the time. It is easy to rely on that gift of intuition. Having this divine gift of intuition is like being connected to the Source personally, and you have your guide throughout the course of life. I will keep a never-ending log of patterns in people's behavior immediately and write it off for what it is. It's like I take daily notes of other people's behavioral and physical habits, and I store them away. When those things are present in other people, I say, "OK, I've seen this before," and immediately put the pieces together. We are so connected to ourselves we use our intuition as a daily guide.

## Mystic Mina

Some people may think that being intuitive is all fun and games, but everything in life has its form of duality. It is beneficial to have the gift of knowing, but it has been times when I wished it didn't. I have learned to turn those hard times into a lesson learned. And keep I on pushing. Some people have this gift but cannot acknowledge it because they are too consumed with the outside noise. Being occupied with people, places, and things make it challenging to know your center and trust your instinct. But being INFJ, that introversion intuition is what comes naturally.

When it comes to the Feeling and Judgement of being an INFJ is all based on extroversion. The feeling part of myself will have the outside world see me as extroverted, but that is not the case. My feelings are rather intense only amongst things I am passionate about. Like love, being creative, comedy and music. Especially when the music comes on, others will view me in totally different light. That Judging aspect is just that. I will judge you on actions and not what you say. Not to bring anyone down, but I'm deciphering if I want you in my world or not.

My extroversion function is powerful when it comes to this. I care about how you treat your family, friends, and those that serve you. I understand that sometimes people will experience different things from different people, but it doesn't matter if you treat me well, but you treat the waiter and janitor like they are lesser than. Because your true character shows in how you treat other people who differ from you. I'm huge on that because a homeless person can probably teach more about life than a college professor can. Everyone's path won't look the same because we are on different journeys in life. According to society standards, if you don't have a long list of traditional accomplishments, some people will deem you inadequate and useless to society. But I know that someone who might differ from those things, might be the one that people look up to for inspiration and guidance

Now being an INFJ isn't all sweet. Being an INFJ isn't just being

# Mystic Mina

a quiet, meek, humble, do-good person. Everyone, including me, has their limits. When I come to a decision, there is no stopping me. I will stand my ground unapologetically. If I allow you into my world giving you the best of me will be an understatement. If you are in my life, it is for a reason, and I will try my best to allow you to experience me the why I want to experience you. And if what I'm receiving doesn't match up with what you said it was going to be, then you will get absolutely nothing, from me.

When the limit is up, and I gave you the most I can give. You will get a completely different experience from me. I have never been the one to exploit people's secrets, tear up clothes, break windows, slash tires or destroy any property. Because I understand there are no rules in revenge. So, I do something more efficient than all those listed, which is the famous "INFJ Door Slam." That door slam is cold coming from someone like me. I have even shocked myself, with it. Now that door slam is just that. I will slam the door on you and your energy. Then I will begin to mourn you, to purge you out of my life.

Some may think that this act is cold and unfair. It is challenging for someone who relies on gut instincts and facts to pretend nothing is wrong. You will get absolutely nothing from me. Because before I even knew there was such thing as a "door slam," I always felt like, once I give to you freely and you misuse me in the process, then I'm done completely. If I let you enter my world, and we both are on the same page, you will receive my best, whatever it is at that time.

At any time, if what I'm giving isn't what you want or respect, I would gladly remove myself from the situation and act as if I wasn't there in the first place, with no love lost. I understand everything isn't for everybody, so I will never be malicious in the act. I just move on gracefully and quietly. People who receive that slam will think it's mainly to hurt them, but that isn't the case at all. It's for my protection, from the pain I feel. Because I will do what I sometimes don't want to do to protect myself. Like I stated previously, I can't change the person who is hurting me, but I can change whether I want you in my life or not.

I can understand why the INFJ is one of the rarest personality traits. People like me are so multiplexed individuals that it is hard sometimes to believe that anyone knows who we really are. Even though I have listed qualities of an INFJ, that is only the surface of uniqueness that people like me have within us. Sometimes I surprise myself with all the different interests, thoughts, and evolutions I have encountered over the years. Every day there is something new I'm experiencing and learning about myself and this world. Being a deep thinker, the possibilities of ideas are endless. There is still alot I have to learn and encounter, but I am forever grateful to have learned from the lessons that life has presented me with so far.

## Chapter Five: Nothing But Love

On social media and reality shows, one thing will go unnoticed time and time again. Everybody claims they want the one thing but will ignore it if it was right in their face. Or a lot of people will say that they don't want it and be highly miserable without it. That one thing can scare someone out of it and have another floating on cloud nine with it. That one thing is love.

Love seems simple enough. It takes little effort to say I love you, easy to do things that seem loving. But real love is much more detailed than that. Love is a rarity that comes for free. Love is not defined by how many gifts you receive, how much money one hands you, or how much someone will allow you to use them. Love is kind, patient, tender, understanding, nurturing, protective and respectful. Looking at fake love displayed on social media will leave

# Mystic Mina

people with distorted ideas on what it is. Love isn't about Gucci, Birkin bags, Lambo trucks, fancy trips, and lavish dinners. Those things are loving, but real love doesn't reside in material things.

Love is many things, and being patient, understanding, caring, nurturing, peaceful, thoughtful, and respectful can build a strong foundation for love to grow. Looks and money have nothing to do with real love. That's why, for some people, if you don't have those qualities listed above, it doesn't matter how much money you have or how attractive you are; they will pay you no mind. That is me. Like I stated previously, those things don't move me at all. Yeah, you can see somebody that's fine and lust after them, but once that feeling is gone, so is everything else.

Love isn't vain or materialistic. Love is the foundation of something greater. Yes, everyone has preferences, but what is the point when those preferences aren't exuding with the kind of love you want and desire If your love for material things persuades your Judgment of loving the soul and essence of someone, then your love is based on something superficial. Money is only a tool or resource needed in this world to survive, and that's it. We have traded the essence of love for worldly possessions. And anyone who ever experienced real love can tell you that love goes beyond this world, space, and time. Money doesn't replace happiness. If it did, then all the millionaires and famous people in this world would live a world overflowed with joy. But we all know that is not the case.

Love has many classifications, but the thing it is not is one-sided. Everybody wants to be loved, but everybody is terrified to do the exact something they desire from people. Love is an energy that needs reciprocation to flourish thoroughly. Without water and sunshine, can flowers survive and grow? Today people will throw disrespect, infidelity, and dishonesty in their relationship and become enraged when the connection is annihilated. Suppose you think a relationship is there for you to take from, and that person is only there to feed your insecurities and boost your ego. In that case, you will automatically disqualify yourself from receiving genuine love anyway. Love can exist so long in this place smothered in unhappiness.

That, again, is a reason why you must make yourself happy and content first. Because what tends to happen is unhappy people will enter relationships and demand their partner to make them happy, which is impossible. In the end, they begin to become unsatisfied with their partner for not making them happy. Then the cycle continues. Those people never realize the main denominator of their unhappiness is themselves. One will never win if one doesn't change within.

I remember, through one phase in my life, I was told, "I didn't have anything besides love to offer." But I know there was a time where love is all we had to survive. Way before the love of material things came along. Love was all people had, and that love allowed them to grow and be able to venture and do different things in life. That's why I love animals so much because no one tells them how to love. Like a lioness protecting her cubs, elephants forming herds for protection, or wolves adjusting placements in the pack to shield the young and the elderly. Even birds work relentlessly to make a nest for their eggs, and it's all out of love. Of course, nature isn't about happy animals and rainbows all of the time, but they still can show love their way time and time again.

Even in past relationships, people tried to win me over with gifts after, total disrespect. But that only went so far with me. Gifts are lovely, but they don't erase the pain you feel, they don't dry the tears away, and they didn't make it easier to sleep at night. Usually, the disrespect appears when they don't respect themselves because once you truly respect yourself, you will appreciate the relationships you have with other people. For example, if you happen to be in a romantic relationship with someone that continuously shows no regard to the relationship you share. That person is dangerous, and they need to be left behind. People who choose to act recklessly have no concern for themselves, and they will handle you the same way. If someone puts themselves in harmful situations, protecting you will be the furthest thing from their mind.

Insecurities and being in survival mode will usually have people behave in such a manner. That's why self-love and true acceptance is imperative for everybody. Having insecurities will drive you to do things that you shouldn't do to feel secure. Being insecure will allow you to be available to anyone at any time. In hopes that they will enter your personal space and make you feel you feel complete and secure. Being insecure will leave you open to anything because boundaries aren't allowed when you're blindly searching for completeness outside of yourself.

So, during this time, it is a given you will suffer more heartbreak and disappointment living life this way. Entertaining nonsense solely because you are too afraid to let it go because if it leaves, you feel you have nothing, will leave you empty and depleted every time. That's why you have to fill up your own cup and give away the residuals and not by continuously leaving your cup open for others to take, hoping they will fill it for you one day.

In a relationship of any kind, if reciprocation of care, honesty, trust, compassion, respect, loyalty, solidarity, understanding, gratitude, and patience isn't present, love wouldn't be either. You can't demand honesty when you don't speak the truth. For someone to care for you, you cannot mishandle them. It is egotistical to demand respect, loyalty, and gratitude from anyone, while you remain inconsiderate, unfaithful, and ungrateful. True love has no place for ego. Love cannot grow where ego resides.

## Chapter Six: Dancing with the Devil

Well, if any empathic people are reading this, I'm sure you know what this feels like firsthand. Even though I tried to use discernment with my relationships, I can honestly say I have done this dance, too, naively. Before I get started, remember this isn't to bash anyone. Everyone on this planet has their life passage, and sometimes we meet unhealed people on our journey of healing, and sometimes we may run into a mirror of our unhealed selves. But never-the-less, there are ways to avoid this dance.

Dancing with the devil is just a metaphor for entertaining low vibrational people for a certain amount of time. This dance will leave you feeling depleted every time. But one word that comes to mind when people hear this subject. The very famous narcissist. Thanks to social media and YouTube, that word has been thrown around very loosely to describe traits in others that we don't like. Automatically you will hear that screamed and written to make the world aware that a narcissist was here, I loved them, and now I'm damaged. It is possible that anyone can have a toxic characteristic or be too egotistical, but that doesn't necessarily make them narcissists. It goes much deeper than that.

Being a narcissist isn't something that's developed overnight, so calling your partner a narcissist due to a disagreement or a negative trait you see in them is a form of exaggeration. Being a narcissist is labeled as a personality disorder. There are ten personality traits, but it might be less depending on what or who you study. In a nutshell, a narcissist has an inflated sense of importance and superiority, requires excessive attention and admiration, and suffers from a severe lack of empathy. To some, those qualities sound like someone is cold, selfish, and insensitive. That is the face they put for the world because they don't want anyone to see them as insecure, afraid, and fragile. Many people say they know what a narcissist is but rarely know the weakness that causes this neurotic behavior.

The narcissist and an unhealed empath can be very similar in different ways. For instance, a narcissist will take; all an empath does is give, a narcissist will always be unsure, an empath will always be there to do the reassuring, a narcissist will love the bomb after a disaster, and an empath will always be there to pick up the pieces. Yes, one can be perceived as unfavorable and the other positive. Still, in this unhealthy relationship, both party's insecurities will be catered to during this time until the Empath gets to drained to the point of no return. Or the narcissist will find another energy source or participant. It's a never-ending story.

Now I know my empaths and compassionate people are like, "How did I play a part in this tango? All I did was try to love on them, and I got hurt. What did I do?' Nothing is wrong with loving someone but not loving yourself enough is where the problem lies. When you must prove your love to someone with no reciprocation, that's a problem. That's a problem when you accept the love bomb gifts because you have been abused physically and emotionally. If the only security you have in a relationship comes from catering to other people's insecurities, that is a problem. It is a problem when you decide to ignore your gift of intuition to make the narcissist comfortable, so they won't be accountable for their actions. I know everything isn't for everybody and you may feel that this dance is enough for you. But if you feel depleted, worn, and used, this dance is painful for you too, but I know sometimes it seems easier to let the dance of toxicity continue rather than stopping the music completely.

    As an empath, there is absolutely no way to stop caring for others deeply. Instead of building a wall up from the world, a simple door will do the trick. I know you may say to yourself a door for a narcissist won't work. That's only if you gave the narcissist a key then decided later you wanted to change the locks because, during this time, the narcissist will feel like you are keeping them away from something that belongs to them, which is when it could lead to extreme measures. You might need a different plan of protection in that case.

But a door is enough to keep them out because they never want to stay where there's no benefit or control. So, you don't hand them anything. Set up personal boundaries and never leave that door open. They don't want to stay anywhere that holds them accountable for their action. Stop accepting the love bombs. They know that is ultimately what you desire. For them to treat you the way you have been begging for, and they give it only long enough to keep the benefits flowing from you to them.

Like I previously stated before that everyone has personal free will to do what they desire. But suppose you are continuously dealing with someone who constantly hurts you emotionally, spiritually, and physically. In that case, there comes a time when you must take personal accountability for allowing yourself to be a victim continuously. Yes, some people encounter some hurt in life, but it becomes a personal choice to stay in the cesspool of a relationship.

Instead of blaming the person hurting you, you need to step back and ask yourself why you keep allowing yourself to stay in this pain? Why do you devalue yourself so much that this treatment is OK? All the wishing's, hoping, praying, and inspirational posts will not change another free-willed individual. You must look and make a change within yourself to get what you desire. The other party may be satisfied with being the way they are, which is perfectly fine for them. Remember, everyone has their path of growth. But you can choose not to endure their course because you have your own life course to pass. Remember, love is not a license for pain, and you can choose yourself at any given time and learn that lessons and blissing's are in goodbyes.

# Mystic Mina

# Chapter Seven: Club Clowning

First off, I love music, so being at the club, felt like home to me. The club is where I used to reside. It didn't matter if it was a Hollywood club, a hole in the wall, the big girl club, strip club gay, or straight and the after-hours. I was everywhere, having the time of life. From 18-30 years of age, a big chunk of my outings club oriented. Since I had no children, I had a lot of free time to turn up for real.

Being a young adult in the 99 and 2000's in Los Angeles, I had a whole heap of fun. During that time, I knew about all the hot spots. People called me like people will use Google today to see where the party was. I had the pleasure to part in the Century Club, Sky Sushi, Club Fever,

Mystic Mina

Club Curves, Dublins, Red Velvet, The Post, Savoy, The Lakewood Hop, Cub Atlas, Shakedown, and the Catch One. Those are only the ones I frequent regularly. I have seen many artists that I still love, from Busta Rhymes, Brandy, Monica, and Faith Evans, to name a few.

It was absolutely nothing for me to spend all of my free to get ready for one night. I would wake up in the morning and get myself together for that night. I would go to the Fox Hills and dash down Slauson to find my outfit, shoes, accessories, and hair for that night, and that could take anywhere from 4-5 hours. Then it's time to do my hair, take a shower, and get ready to go. Leave the house around 8 to get to my destination. Pull up by 9:30 to pre-game in the car and walk into the club around 10 pm. I partied all night until the famous "It's time to go" song will come on. Then after it's over, head on out to Tams, Fabulous Burgers, Denny's, Jack in the Crack, or hit up one of that bacon-wrapped hot dog vendors on the corner. Then it's time to

# Mystic Mina

regroup and go home, get some sleep and do the same thing again.

Each year that passed by became less fun. At the time, I chucked it up, do to me getting older. But one night, I went out by myself, just hit the dance floor for a couple of songs, and to vibe out alone. I paid the usual $20 cover charge at the time. I got my typical Vodka and Cranberry, sat back, and watched. Then it seemed like I had an out-of-body experience, my reality turned into a slow-motion movie, and I never looked at the club the same. I had all of these downloads come to me instantly. It was just my time to wake up for that club slumber.

I started to realize how much money I spent on the club. Between the outfits, hairdos, cover charge, drinks, and VIPs, I can honestly say I have spent up and over tens of thousands of dollars in the club. Not to mention the gas prices and the wear and tear I put on my car because I was the driver I often went. And leaving with absolutely nothing to show for it and making the club rich than getting into my financed vehicle and drive to my apartment. I realized I spent someone's life savings on just having a good time.

Then I realized the people I partied with; we were all stagnant in life. And that was a massive problem for me. There had to be something wrong to still be in the mental space I was in my twenties at in at thirty. Of course, I always had dreams I wanted to accomplish, but my dreams seemed impossible while behaving in this manner. Yes, I always had a "good job with benefits," but I couldn't financially afford to be wasting money like that. Being financially independent and financially abundant is two different things. No kind of abundance was going to come from that behavior.

There had to be something wrong with me to go against my dreams. I had to be running away from something in my life. To spend all of the money I received from a job that I wasn't passionate about, party every weekend with strangers. I had much more to be concerned about. I was overweight for one, and I should have been more vigilant about my health. Even if you are a big healthy person, the bigger you are, the more strain you will put on your body throughout the years. This isn't to bash anyone because I am still conquering a healthier lifestyle, but I am on a better path of health, being almost 100lbs down.

I had no kids, and I should have been spending my money wisely by investing, having a passive income, starting a business, or just putting myself in a position to become more abundant in life. While in the club, I started noticing all the money that voluntarily contributed to support someone else's dream. I know everybody has to make a living in this world; it's our earthly right. I wanted financial abundance and for flashy reasons. But I understand the more financially secure you are, the freer you become. Plus, I wanted more out of life than to be bonded to "9 to 5" for most of my life. To retire with crumbs and a couple of years of life to spare. I knew that I wanted and deserved more than what that aspect of life had to offer.

I had a lot to reflect on in my life. Wasting time and money in places where I'm not growing from emotionally and spirituality, wasn't a place a needed to be to get to my destination. Now, this is does not mean that I will dismiss my love of dancing all together. It will just be in the proper time and place, an event that I could afford financially and emotionally. This was a big moment in life that allowed me to become more self-aware and self-driven.

## Chapter Eight: In Hermit Mode

It took time for me to come to the place I am in right now. Even though I am still not where I want to be, I'm ecstatic I have grown from the locations I once was. I stopped myself in my tracks to evaluate where I was in life and what I had to do to get to my destination. Conquering my shadow work just me, myself, and I, duct off away from the outside world. Most of the time, the people who tend to take care of everyone rarely have time to heal themselves. So, I made a conscious decision to choose myself first, but I had to complete a couple of steps to get there.

I had to learn to say no, even though that sounds easy for certain people, but by being so empathic, I can feel empathy for others without showing the same concern to myself. I mean, being constantly on the go was an understatement. I was everywhere people needed me to be. I was always available for advice, transportation, celebration, and everything else, but I noticed they didn't meet me with the same reciprocity. I decided to love myself more. I know now that self-love is just that, and if you don't give that to yourself, no one will be able to neither. 30 was a big breakthrough year for me to see everything that kept me blind. My reality turned upside down, and I saw things differently. I then realized the problems I was fighting weren't my own to be concerned about in the first place. When I realized that, I knew something had to change.

I started to love myself, honestly. Even though I proclaimed I

## Mystic Mina

did, I would do something that goes against my better Judgment in the next breath. I fell in love with myself completely, flaws and all. One thing about me is that I have always been very optimistic, and I have always been that kind of person that looks at flaws as just a part of myself that needs some fine-tuning that I need to change. I began to walk away peacefully from things that didn't serve me anymore. I took a step back in my life to disengage for a bit. Just to get familiar with who I had surrounding me and focus on what I was allowing in my life. Usually, when someone makes life decisions taking a step back to recognize your next move is the best. It is a lot easier for someone looking at a fight to come up with specific solutions better than the person in the fight, who only has his eye on the opponent, in certain situations. To love me better than I already was, I had to let a lot of things go.

The first thing, I stopped going out so much. Every weekend you will find me out, functioning, trying to mask the dysfunction I felt within. I

# Mystic Mina

mean, my credit was jacked. I had no kids while overweight, just wasting money on club admissions, VIP section, outfits, alcohol, and everything in between. When you are young, you will experience this world in different phases, just being young, wild, and free. But when you are over 30, and you realized you must face those mental and physical restraints you had in your twenties, you start to view the world differently. Coming from where I'm from, I understand people celebrating just because they survived another day, but I began to realize that it is so easy to get caught in that same cycle of doing the same thing in your 20s, 30s, 40, even in your 50s. I wanted more out of life. I realized I could achieve my desires once I focused on bettering myself.

The second thing I did was stop being under the influence so much. I remember back when a bottle of wine, a big bottle of wine, was nothing for me to drink on a weekday after work. That habit can become so ritualistic, without realizing it, you start to think this is just a thing to do. Not realizing the alcohol is there to help

## Mystic Mina

you forget your ailments and it's not helping your situations. But I understand completely, you attend work all day dealing the frustrations of life and you go home to escape your day in a bottle. Then you will continue this everyday and when the weekend arrives you reward yourself with some more liquor and the cycle will continue next week. Now don't get me wrong, I still will have a drink from time to time, but my whole social outing and alone time are not focused on how drunk or tipsy I can get.

Plus, I can't vouch for anybody else, but drinking became more challenging for me the older I got. Having a hangover in your 20's feels way different when you are older. Personally, having those all-day headaches, with sensitive eyes and a queasy stomach, wasn't fun at all. Especially if you're trying to become a better person for yourself, always having a hangover will get you nowhere. Even when I didn't have a hangover, my body still notified me that I was doing too much either by having acid reflux or just my urine not being as clear as it should be. I'm grateful that I never had high blood pressure because mixing that with alcohol is a disaster waiting to happen.

I'm not even going to go deep about the excess calories and food craving you get while drinking. Stopping at a food stand after having 3 to 5 drinks can add on at least 2,000 calories on your day, not realizing you need to lose 3500 calories, just to lose one pound. And you have no clear judgment while being drunk. Drinking will often have you more accessible to people or situations that you probably wouldn't indulge in with a sober mind. There is no way you can make life decisions while drowning yourself in a bottle of alcohol.

Another thing I stopped was involving myself in other people's emotional emergencies. Don't get me wrong. I can be that listening ear if needed. Still, I'm talking about that emotional manipulation people will often do to get you involved emotionally in their problems. Then their emergency becomes yours because now you are emotionally invested. This doesn't apply to everyone that needs help. This only to the ones who always seem to need help. This help isn't usually due to unforeseen circumstances. This kind of help where the other person made a wrong decision, not regarding the specific possibility, messed up the whole situation. Still, when they come to you, they make it seem as if it is now your responsibility to fix this problem. There will be no sincerity when those people are asking for your help. Their asking will always sound demeaning, controlling, and forceful. Because you are their last hope, they will pull every manipulative act out of their hat to get on board.

The best way I started handling this situation is not to answer immediately. I will state that I need more time to think about this because being emotionally driven gives you no time to sit and analyze this situation. You will just act on their feelings without deciphering if this was the most appropriate thing to do. So, I just take the emotions out of the equation to take some time to think it over. So, if it means me helping them

## Mystic Mina

will hurt myself in return. I'm opting out to choose me. Usually, by that time, the one who was asking will be so furious that you didn't make an emotional move, they probably wouldn't want the help anymore because whatever they said didn't make you jump to the rescue. They probably will have a problem with you, too.

One thing about being in hermit mode is meditation is extremely necessary just to get peace and clarity. It is impossible to get in tune with your true self while occupied by outside influences and noise. Serenity will become so important in your life to the extent, and you will begin to question how you functioned with all of the chaos that kept you surrounded. When some people hear meditation, they will probably have a mental vision of something or someone with nothing to do with proper meditation. You do not need to be on a yoga mat in the woods to do this.

All you need is peace, that's it. Whether in bed, in the tub, or your car, you need space and time to get in tune with your true self. Many people

## Mystic Mina

don't realize today they are so consumed with other things and people because they are afraid to dwell in their thoughts. During that time, all of the pain and trauma of the past. Accompanied by your bad choices will continue to flood on in. It becomes effortless for people to become so overwhelmed, so they in return, will begin drowning out their thoughts with food, substances and then start a toxic cycle of dissociation of their reality. And that is why shadow work is also necessary to map out those emotions. All in all, you need to meditate, have peace, serenity, and a moment of silence to heal from within and grow from places you are currently locked in.

Be aware that being in hermit mode isn't easy, especially if you are always on every scene. Some people will judge you when you decide not to participate in the things you used to do just because you will become the oddball out. You want to be able to hit every party, get drunk every night, and entertain the same people as you did before. You will not be available to highlight your new wig, outfit, or destination. Some people will not understand that. It's not because something is wrong with doing those things, but to get into certain places and through phases in life, you will have to let go of what is familiar to get to your new destination. You will never get anything new in life, repeating the same cycles of your past. To get something you never had, you have to do something you have never done. Getting to this place isn't easy, but the rewards will be worth it so much. It will be tough to go against yourself once you know how to evolve into the most excellent version of yourself.

## Chapter Nine: Being Safe in Your Shadows

Shadow work is a scary word for many people, but to completely heal shadow work is imperative. It will be never-ending as well. If you encounter trials and tribulations throughout this life, you will need to work to make it through those times efficiently. You must face those things that trigger you head-on to conquer them. Locking them away in the closet will not make them go away. Masking them with people, places, or things will not make it easier. You will encounter more problems than your origin\al shadow from the beginning. Doing this will require a lot of courage, but you will be reward with a lot of clarity.

I went into Hermit mode previously. During that time, I had to face certain truths about myself. Seeing yourself through a cracked mirror isn't a pretty sight. Especially when you think you look like a perfect picture. I had to stop pretending everything was fine and clean up my mess. I had to forgive the others in my life that wronged me. I know people hate to forgive, but forgiveness isn't for them is designed for you.

The burden of unforgiveness is a heavy load to carry. Every day, you are reminded of what they did or didn't do to you. Every day you walk around hating them. Every day you chose not to forgive them. Notice the person who can't forgive is the one holding the responsibility of the unforgiven. If there was any way to give that worry and the load of unforgiveness to the party that it belongs to, then not forgiving will be easy.

But that is not how life works. So, the person who caused you not to forgive is possibly living a happy, unconcerned life while you walk the weight of their mistakes seven days a week. Just that act alone is tiring within itself. It is bad enough that you already endured pain, so why do you want to hold on to it. Once you start forgiving, you stop reliving the occurrence that caused you pain.

Then you will start to realize that pain doesn't belong to you. Yes, things occurred in your life, and you felt the result of that. Once you understand the pain that you endured was only the residuals of what was inside of the person that caused you the pain, you will become freer. We often see people functioning on an adult level during life, like having a job, their place, kids, and a marriage. And society will assume that every parent has all the answers, every partner will love you, and your friends will never betray you. In a perfect world, that sounds easy enough. But we know no matter how together we look, there are things we endure and haven't gotten over in life. It becomes an issue when we forget that everybody in this life is doing the same thing.

They are just navigating their way through this thing called life. They live with unresolved problems that become other people's issues because they have no idea how to deal with them themselves. Yes, there may be times when someone deliberately harms you, but please be aware for that type of energy to transfer to you, it had to be inside of them.

You will never receive a sunflower from a rose bush. It doesn't have anything to produce a sunflower. And it is the same with people. If love is inside of me, that is what you will receive, and if hurt is inside, then pain is what you will receive. A healed person knows that their issues are their own and will sort through them accordingly without placing anything or blame on someone else.

Another part of shadow work deals with the scariest part, yourself. You may be asking how one can be afraid of themselves. When you realize that a lot of the pain you endured in this life was your fault. That's a hard pill to swallow. You can't put that reckless behavior on anyone but yourself. You made the wrong decisions in your life that caused your downfall. Like putting yourself in situations, where the only outcome will be detrimental to yourself. That can make you start questioning your sanity and begin to ask questions like, "what in the world was I thinking?" I can't believe I did that!

Believe it or not, that part is a part of life. Everybody is navigating life on the information that they have at the moment. That is why learning is fundamental. The more you know, the more choices you have to choose from, but if you continue to stay in the same spaces, you will keep getting the same results. Learning to forgive during this stage is the only way to get through. Understand that no one is perfect, not even you. Everyone deals with these situations in life. But what makes people different from each other is the choices they make despite of the pain.

Some people will accept living in their pain, and others choose to get out of it. Others think they are getting out of their misery by dismissing it but doing that only leads to more pain. It is painful to feel the sores of your past. It is like reliving that moment over again. And you are put back in the same confinement of pain. So, you choose to forget the process and the pain and start pretending that you are fine, and nothing phases you. Then you might begin to drown your pain in alcohol or food, numbing your pain with drugs, start throwing your pain on other people, or start masking it with physical gratification.

Living a facade is very easy to do today. All you have to do is find the right picture to post with a few memes and with a couple of fake destinations, and you have a perfect life. But how is that beneficial to you? You pretend that everything is good, but you cry yourself to sleep once everything is off or shut down. You must choose between facing your pain or returning to the coping mechanism that causes you more pain. Either way, your pain has turned into an addiction, and now it seems impossible to get past this phase. That's why Shadow Work is imperative because whether you decide to face yourself, you will still have to face the problems you placed on yourself.

Mystic Mina

## Chapter Ten: The Gift in Gratefulness

I know everyone knows about being grateful. We are often thankful for our looks, material possessions, and social status in today's society. But those things are easy to be grateful for. The gifts of gratefulness will always be there when tangible and material items aren't accessible. To be endlessly abundant, you will have to be genuinely grateful.

On a typical day, the majority will have a day that looks like this. You and your family will get yourself together to start your day. You get dressed, eat, and then it is off to your car to head to your destination. You finish your day, and you and your family will go home, clean up, eat dinner and get ready for your next day to begin. Throughout that day, how many things are you grateful for? Are you grateful for life? Your ability to see, hear and speak. Or just to be grateful for your strength and mind.

## Mystic Mina

Be grateful for your perseverance to stand firm through those trying times. Or just being grateful for the trees, birds, and the Sun.

Throughout this life, people tend to get caught up in unimportant things. Stuff that doesn't matter. Everyone is worried about their clothes, the car they drive, the money in their pocket, and their physical characteristics. But when all of those things disappear, then what do you have? Do you have integrity? Are you honest? Do you know the meaning of true love? Or do you use people as pawns to win the games you are playing? If you are using people to win, then you have already lost, and you will receive only what your energy is putting out. Energy is a revolving door, and what you give out, you will get back.

Energy has a lot to do with gratefulness. Suppose you walk around with negative energy evolving in life. Your outlook in life will be just that. It is impossible to be in a place of gratefulness, blinded by negativity. Your view will be so distorted you will not be able to see the truth right in front of you. Because seeing the world through a negative lens will leave your sight foggy and distorted. There are ways to change this, but you must be willing to do the work for that change. Try to look on the other side of the spectrum and see how your life changes. Looking at things through a positive light, has nothing to perfection. You must choose to be happy whether if things are perfect or not. Only, when you do this will you be able to live a beautiful and grateful life.

## Chapter Eleven: Healed from My Mothers Pain

My mother was born into a family of 13 children to parents who were sharecroppers in the deep, deep south of Alabama. Only a couple generations removed from slavery, my mother recalls hearing her grandmother tell her stories of hearing runaway slaves as a little girl. My mother became a wife and a mother at the age of 17. She birthed her first child at the house with midwives to assist her creation to this world. My mother will let you quickly know, "I had a baby, a husband with nothing in my pocket." My mother never finished her high school education, but one thing my mother could do without a doubt or question during any time or place, was survive. Her stories of survival saved my life.

My mother's stories were never dull. That could be a whole book within itself. But whether if she was right, wrong, or indifferent. She often shared her life experiences with me, and for that, I will be forever thankful. When your parents talk to you as a child, you often wonder what they are talking about. Even if I didn't understand at that moment, something inside me let me know that I needed the information she gave me. With me fully developed before the age of 12, she talked to me about boys, sex, and life, maybe around 9. She stated she wanted me to get the correct information instead of being misled in the streets. Especially since her mother told her, if you talk to a boy by yourself, you will get pregnant. She wanted to equip me with information about life and the people in it.

Even though we lived in a rough neighborhood, my home life wasn't of that. She would often give me my own money to hold because she didn't want me to be impressed by a man flashing a few dollars, and I go off running. She always told me I was beautiful and deserved to be loved, but that doesn't mean everyone will love me. She let me know that just because someone says I love you or does something loving, they might be setting me up to use me. I even remember going out to the club while

Mystic Mina

I was living with her, and her favorite thing was to watch America's Most Wanted. It never failed I would be walking out of the door, and she would say, "Ok baby, you be careful because I was watching Americas Most Wanted, where this lady met this FINE man at the club, he bought her a drink, took her home and killed her. But you have fun tonight". My mother was loving, but she didn't sugarcoat anything, and she has never been afraid to speak her mind, which remains the same to this day.

I have learned so many things in life from her. Just her stories of the racial tensions, her endless jobs working in fields, factories, and hotels from Alabama to California, she always instilled in me the importance of being self-resilient. But the one thing she carved in my head is love. She always told me that love doesn't hurt. Coming from a woman who survived an abusive relationship that would be too graphic for regular TV, I knew I had to listen. Someone who truly loves you wouldn't want to hurt you because hurting you will be hurting them. I have come to learn life can hurt when you love someone, but that sometimes is inevitable. But I do understand that hurting someone you love continuously isn't love at all. It might be you love the convenience that this person gives you, but that isn't love.

My mother wasn't a saint, but she has always been an empathic and compassionate person, even through her mistakes. I often remember the times she would give money or food to the homeless, and right after, she would turn to say to me, "I don't mind helping people, they are still someone else's child, and if my children were in need, I would want someone to do the same for you." She would cook up those down south homemade soul food dinners and give out plates to everybody. I remember we had a man in the neighborhood that was always around like Eziel on Friday, and whenever he was around, she made sure to gift him plates. My mother would give out so many rides to people, take them everywhere, for a little or nothing, just out of the kindness of her heart. Every month, she would take some of her siblings for their routine errands, even when she was almost physically incapable.

## Mystic Mina

She has opened her door to so many people. Our house was a haven for some. If you needed some food, money, advice, a bath, or somewhere to stay rent-free, she made it happen, that included our family, her friends, and mine. She stuck through some family member's jail bids, sending money orders, accepting collect calls, boxes, and letters. My mother would post-pone a bill she had due to help others in need. She would give out so much, including money. Out of all the things she has done for people, she hasn't received reciprocity. For all of those reasons I am big on boundaries today.

I sometimes understand the people that do the most are the people that need the most help. Sometimes I fall short myself, still believing that she is as solid and resilient as she was 20 or 30 years ago because it is difficult to look at her in any other way, but her strength still resides in her, even in her later years. My mother still holds on to her independence, like a ninja holding a sword in a fight. But I see the times when she is hurting or questions why people continue to use her for something they already have.

Mystic Mina

I am too flawed, and I am not perfect, and there is no way I could repay my mother for everything she has instilled in me. I know what it feels like to be the only one making things happen, being the only one pouring out more than you are receiving, not having a choice to break down or stop going because if you don't handle it, nobody will. I have come to the realization that we are so different but very much the same. So due to my mother's pain, I will continue to stand in my truth of boundaries and be true to myself and only to those who do the same for me. Because now I understand that once I'm fully healed, she will be too.

## CONCLUSION

Life, Lessons, and Love are very essential to me. Throughout the years of disappointment, heartbreak, and betrayal. One thing has stood evident with me, and that is me. I don't know how to be anything but that. Growing up and in adulthood, I never really felt understood based on how I think. I remember being told that I had nothing to offer besides love. But I know with love that anything can become prosperous. Once you really learn to love, you can start loving yourself, start living in love and begin to see life through a different lens.

Proper understanding isn't about what happened to you but comprehending the lesson of that act is where true understanding stands. In life, there are some things that we don't understand. A lot of time during life, we get stuck in the experiences that happened to us, and we then will begin to claim those things as our life and live as such. Remember, we can't change what others do, but we can change what we continue to endure.

## Mystic Mina

Even though I could take of myself financially, being materialistic was never a concern of mine. Living in my city, that could seem quite odd. I have always been quiet, and I have often been overlooked, misunderstood, or judged wrongly because of that. My mind is always running, and I know they say that it is two sides to every story, but I can see twelve. The ideas and thoughts I have or endless. Even though I went to college but never finished, some may look at me as being incompetent. But my thirst for learning allowed me to educate myself in and out of a classroom setting.

This is me opening a small window inside of my introverted world. Imagine a average house that everyone walks by, but this house has a unique window. It has loud colors around it with glitter thrown all over the frame, with birds sitting on the ledge, accompanied by plants and crystals charging in the sun, with music blasting from it, with the ability to have the ambiance of peace and serenity nearby. The closer you get to it; you notice that the house isn't average at all. It is a whole world behind that window with many

# Mystic Mina

rooms that exude love, creativity, passion, dancing, laughter, wisdom, and beauty that no one knows about, which can make you wonder why you passed it up in the first place. My house might seem a little different, and it may never be perfect. But it is imperfectly mine and I love it that way.

Everybody isn't famous, but everyone has a story. I'm not just sharing a piece of my story for the media to read, but also for myself to remember. Throughout the years, no matter how good you are doing, there will be something in your subconscious mind that will make you doubt yourself. Not because you cannot complete this task but stepping in unknown territory can have anyone fear failure. In that time, you must remember to remind yourself, that you are good enough and the only thing standing in your way, is yourself. So, continue to live in your truth, follow your passion, and watch true abundance overflow into your life.

## Acknowledgments

First, I would like to thank, GOD, for all the love, guidance, and protection I have received throughout my life. I would like to thank my family and friends that genuinely love and support me. I'm also thankful for the love of my life, my twin flame, my wife, I love you beyond time.

## About the Author

Isha' Mina was born and raised in Los Angeles, CA. She attended Los Angeles Trade-Technical College for Business Administration and Cosmetology. Being a County of Los Angeles employee for over 15 years and being an entrepreneur, she decided to incorporate her passion for writing into her life. Realizing she had a story to share about her

## Mystic Mina

emotions, self-discovery, and life experiences. She enjoys helping others, laughing hysterically, being a profound music lover, and thinking outside of the box. While being behind a desk for most of her life, she decided it was time for her to stand in her creativity and authenticity.

www.ingramcontent.com/pod-product-compliance
Lightning Source LLC
Chambersburg PA
CBHW071459160426
43195CB00013B/2163